Postcards fro

D0517271

TREASURES IN THE TRUNK

Quilts of the Oregon Trail

Mary Bywater Cross

RUTLEDGE HILL PRESS

NASHVILLE, TENNESSEE

Published in Nashville, Tennessee, by Rutledge Hill Press, Inc., 211 Seventh Avenue North, Nashville, Tennessee 37219. Distributed in Canada by H. B. Fenn and Company Ltd., Mississauga, Ontario.

ISBN: 1-55853-230-7

Design by Harriette Bateman

Printed in Mexico

1 2 3 4 5 6 7 8 9 — 97 96 95 94 93

INTRODUCTION

Rachel has found an old discarded copper kettle along the roadside, not too bruised she thinks. And as she walks westward she runs a needle and thread through squares of old fabric, storing each stitched piece inside the kettle hanging from her arm like a handbag. She tells Allen she'll have enough of these pieces sewn by the end of the trip to make a quilt. He agrees. That's about all they will have—a kettle and a quilt—but it's worth it.[1]

Like many others, teenage Rachel Bond and her husband, Allen, pioneers of 1853, made their way to Oregon with a wagon train although they themselves did not have money, wagon, oxen, or other supplies. Like other young women of the nineteenth century, Rachel was raised to be supportive of her husband's dreams, taught to create a home-like environment wherever she was, and was eagerly determined to make the migration journey successfully.

The quilts made by the women who traveled the Oregon Trail were a natural outlet for the expression of that experience. These women walked or rode five to twenty miles a day for several months. They experienced new landscapes, new cultures, new people, challenges, and threats. They played new roles that would have a lasting influence on them.

---

[1] Pete Peterson, *Our Wagon Train is Lost,* Eugene, Oregon: New American Gothic, 1975, p. 20.

The quilts in this small postcard collection and those in *Treasures in the Trunk*, from which these were taken, are a record of the migration from East to West. They reflect the preparation and "leave-taking" from family and friends, the six months of living outdoors, and the reliance on both human ingenuity and divine guidance.

By quilting while traveling the Oregon Trail, women were able to enjoy sharing fabrics, patterns, and designs with others. Once settled, their quilting continued to reflect the people, places, and experiences of the Trail.

It was 150 years ago that courageous pioneer women such as Rachel Bond traveled the Oregon Trail. The quilts they made reflected that experience for their own satisfaction, for the benefit of their children or grandchildren who might not have traveled the Trail, and now for our own generation.

POKE STALK (82″ x 76″, 1845) Elizabeth Currier Foster (1832-1921) came over the Oregon Trail in 1846 with her brother, sister, and brother-in-law. This originally designed appliqué quilt, based on a plant native to the East but non-existent in the West, was packed in her trunk for the seven-month journey.
Collection of the Schminck Museum, Lakeview, Oregon

From Treasures in the Trunk © 1993 Mary Bywater Cross

Rutledge Hill Press, Nashville, Tennessee

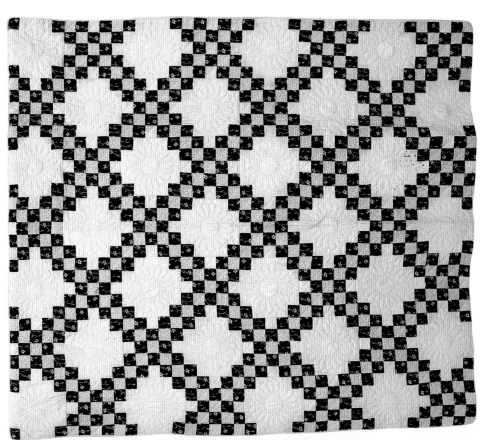

DOUBLE IRISH CHAIN I **(80″ x 68″, 1852)** In 1846, Elizabeth Currier Foster (1832-1921) brought the fabric in her trunk for this migration theme quilt. She made it in 1852 after her marriage and the birth of four babies, two of whom died. *Collection of the Schminck Museum, Lakeview, Oregon*

Rutledge Hill Press, Nashville, Tennessee

ROSE OF SHARON (90″ x 80″, 1854) Close examination reveals the secrets of this quilt. Four of the blocks match, indicating they were completed at the same time by the same person. A fifth block varies in the style of blooms, while the remaining four have different fabrics and buds instead of blooms. Elizabeth Currier Foster (1832-1921) brought the blocks and fabric in her trunk in 1846 and finished the quilt in 1854. *Collection of the Schminck Museum, Lakeview, Oregon*

From Treasures in the Trunk © *1993 Mary Bywater Cross*

Rutledge Hill Press, Nashville, Tennessee

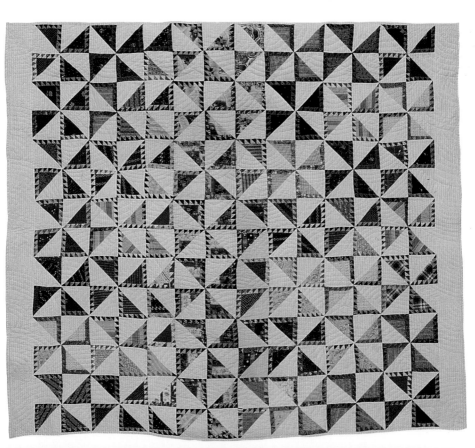

FLYING STAR (82″ x 72″, begun c. 1844, finished 1910) According to family history, Elizabeth Currier Foster (1832-1921) brought the center rows of this quilt in her trunk in 1846. The finished quilt is a demonstration of her determination to complete the project, which she did in 1910. *Collection of the Schminck Museum, Lakeview, Oregon*

From Treasures in the Trunk © *1993 Mary Bywater Cross*

Rutledge Hill Press, Nashville, Tennessee

MEXICAN LILY (86″ x 84″, begun 1854, finished 1915) Elizabeth Currier Foster (1832-1921) brought the pattern for this quilt in cut fabric pieces in her trunk over the Oregon Trail in 1846. The fabrics match those of two other quilts made by Elizabeth during her long career of quiltmaking. *Collection of the Schminck Museum, Lakeview, Oregon*

From Treasures in the Trunk © 1993 Mary Bywater Cross

Rutledge Hill Press, Nashville, Tennessee

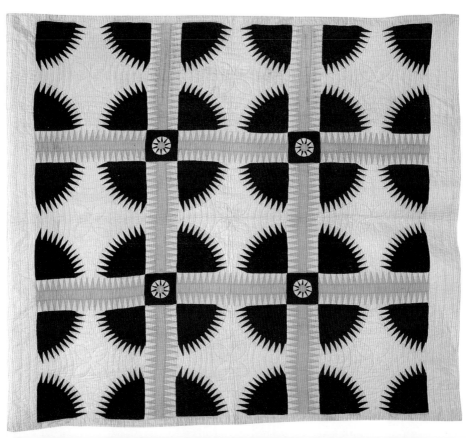

WRIGHT WHEEL OF FORTUNE (82½" x 72", 1848)
The quilt's name reflects the migration experience of
Lavina Elizabeth Frazier Wright (1829-1912) on one
of the first wagon trains over the Trail in 1843. Her
family's journey, under the leadership of Jesse
Applegate, was especially long and difficult because
the route needed to be cleared as they went along.
Collection of the Molalla Area Historical Society,
Molalla, Oregon

From Treasures in the Trunk © *1993 Mary Bywater Cross*

Rutledge Hill Press, Nashville, Tennessee

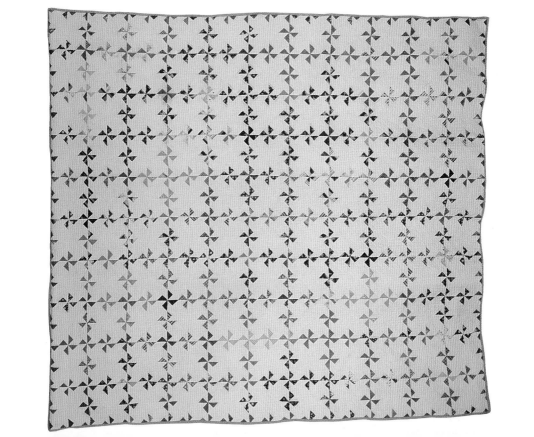

PIN WHEEL (81¾" x 77½", 1849) Sarah Koontz Glover (1803-1885) pieced the small blocks of this quilt while crossing the plains in 1849. The wheel motif is symbolic of the sense of movement in the slow-moving wagons and the constant blowing winds. *Collection of the Oregon Historical Society, Portland, Oregon*

From Treasures in the Trunk © *1993 Mary Bywater Cross*

Rutledge Hill Press, Nashville, Tennessee

WHEEL (83¾″ x 71½″, begun 1849, finished later)
According to family history, Sarah Koontz Glover (1803-1885) pieced this "wheel pattern" quilt "crossing the plains in 1849." Further study indicates she finished it when she returned to quilting after the death of her husband in 1872. *Private collection*

From Treasures in the Trunk © *1993 Mary Bywater Cross*

Rutledge Hill Press, Nashville, Tennessee

FLASHING MINNOW (79½" x 70", 1852) The maker of this quilt Lucinda Cox Brown Allen Spencer (1816-1888) used her needle skills to earn enough money to purchase a land claim after the death of her husband on the Oregon Trail. *Private collection*

From Treasures in the Trunk © 1993 Mary Bywater Cross

Rutledge Hill Press, Nashville, Tennessee

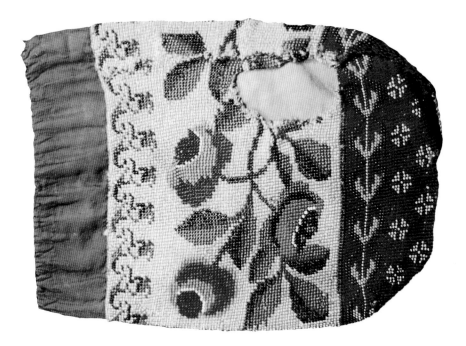

BEADED BAG The vacant space on this beaded bag was created by Elizabeth Currier Foster (1832-1921) when she cut a rose to be placed on the grave of Salita Jane Henderson, who died of an overdose of medicine on the Oregon Trail in 1846. *Collection of the Schminck Museum, Lakeview, Oregon*

From Treasures in the Trunk © 1993 Mary Bywater Cross

Rutledge Hill Press, Nashville, Tennessee

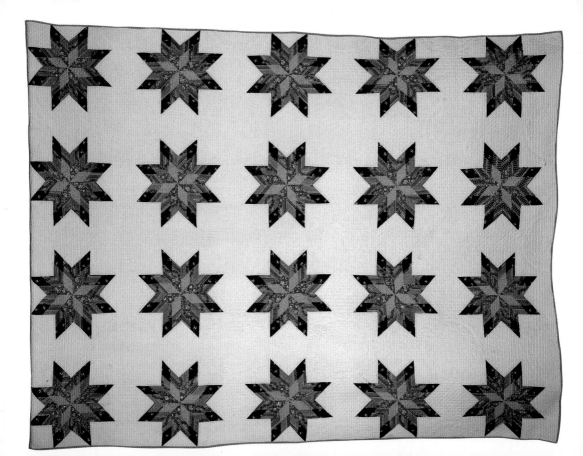

STAR **(91″ x 70″, c. 1830)** Jane Lieb Riggs (1814-1874) brought this pieced Star quilt of early American fabrics dating between 1800-1830 with her on the ill-fated journey across the plains that took the lives of her husband and only daughter in 1851. She settled with her four sons in Polk County where the young men built her a four-room house with a double fire-place. *Collection of the Oregon Historical Society, Portland, Oregon*

From Treasures in the Trunk © *1993 Mary Bywater Cross*

Rutledge Hill Press, Nashville, Tennessee

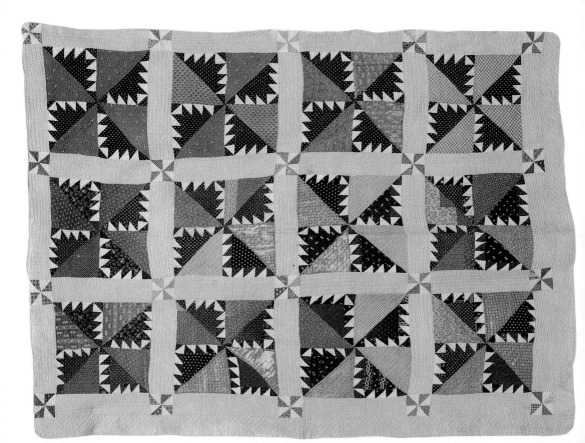

DELECTABLE MOUNTAINS (87″ x 66½″, c. 1840)
The family of Lucinda Ann Leonard Worth, the
maker's granddaughter, treasures this Delectable
Mountains quilt as a symbol of her survival of The
Lost Wagon Train in 1853. As evidence of the impor-
tance of the Oregon Trail in their lives, this quilt has
been cherished for five generations from the maker
Cahterine Purdom to the great-great-granddaughter.
Private collection

From Treasures in the Trunk © *1993 Mary Bywater Cross*

Rutledge Hill Press, Nashville, Tennessee

SETTING SUN **(86″ x 71½″, c. 1840)** Documentation states this quilt was made from the baby dresses of George Hamilton Greer (1836-1928). Margaret Hamilton Greer (1808-1895) came from Ireland in 1831 with her husband James so that he could work in the Philadelphia textile industry. The fabrics are most likely from those early mills. Turning to farming, the family came to Oregon in 1852 from Missouri. *Collection of the Oregon Historical Society, Portland, Oregon*

From Treasures in the Trunk © 1993 Mary Bywater Cross

Rutledge Hill Press, Nashville, Tennessee

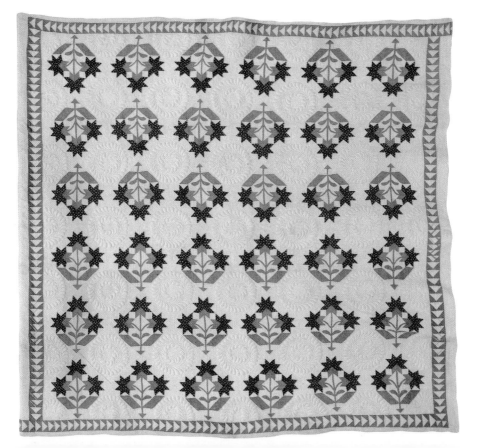

PEONY WITH FLYING GEESE BORDER (80″ x 78″, 1848) This masterpiece quilt combining pieced and appliqué construction techniques with elaborate quilting and stuffwork is signed and dated "S.W. 1848" in the lower right corner. It was made by either Grace Weaver (1815-1885) or Susanna Weaver (1787-1872) and brought across the plains in 1852 as a treasure for Susannah, the ten-year-old daughter of Hans and Harriet Bigham Weaver. *Collection of the Douglas County Museum of History and Natural History, Roseburg, Oregon*

From Treasures in the Trunk © 1993 Mary Bywater Cross

Rutledge Hill Press, Nashville, Tennessee

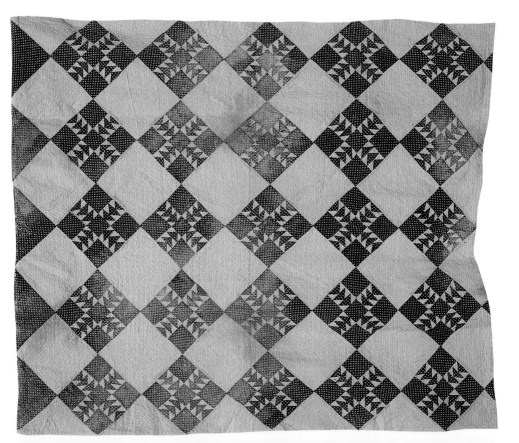

ROAD TO CALIFORNIA (**73″ x 63″, c. 1850**) The pieced triangles of indigo blue and white represent the "wanderings" of Charles Drain. He left his wife Nancy Gates Ensley Drain (1817-?), who made the quilt, and family in Indiana to go to the gold fields. He returned home and brought them to Oregon in 1852. *Private collection*

From Treasures in the Trunk © *1993 Mary Bywater Cross*

Rutledge Hill Press, Nashville, Tennessee

ROSE VARIATION (**90″ x 90″, c. 1850**) This Rose
Variation appliqué quilt is one of at least seventeen
quilts attributed to Zeralda Carpenter Bones Stone
(1822-1914) as a celebration of her life. New clues
identify it as a wedding quilt for her first marriage
before her 1853 journey from Missouri with her sec-
ond husband. *Collection of the Oregon Historical
Society, Portland, Oregon*

From Treasures in the Trunk © *1993 Mary Bywater Cross*

Rutledge Hill Press, Nashville, Tennessee

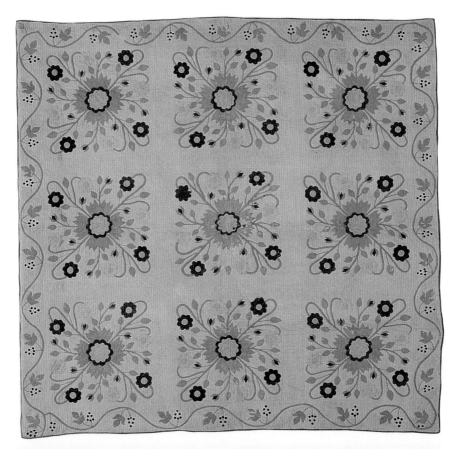

OREGON ROSE (**88½" x 84", 1851**) This is the classic Oregon Trail quilt, made by the friends, neighbors, and relatives of Jacob and Sarah Robbins, before their migration west in 1852. It has their names, date, initials, and quilted symbols of grapevines, hearts, and wheels appealing to God for Divine Guidance on their journey. *Collection of the Molalla Historical Society, Molalla, Oregon*

From Treasures in the Trunk © 1993 Mary Bywater Cross

Rutledge Hill Press, Nashville, Tennessee

TULIP (85½" x 77", 1851-1852) This appliqué quilt made by Illinois friends and neighbors of Lucinda Powell Propst is a treasured heirloom from the fateful 1852 journey that took the lives of both Lucinda and her husband Andrew, leaving five orphaned children. *Private collection*

From Treasures in the Trunk © 1993 Mary Bywater Cross

Rutledge Hill Press, Nashville, Tennessee

WANDERING FOOT (**82″ x 74″, 1852**) The pattern celebrates the American virtue of striking out on one's own to settle in the new Oregon Territory. It was probably pieced on the trail by Amelia Grimsley Morris (1826-1912) who brought the bolt of fabric for the solid blocks in her wagon in 1851. *Private collection*

From Treasures in the Trunk *© 1993 Mary Bywater Cross*

Rutledge Hill Press, Nashville, Tennessee

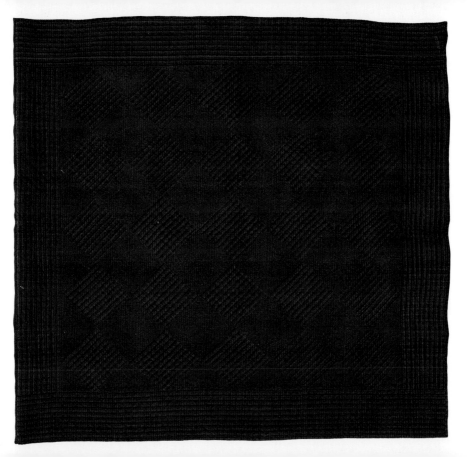

RUNNING SQUARES (81″ x 77″, c. 1860) This Aurora Colony quilt was made by Emma Wagner Giesy (1835-1882), the only female member of the Bethel scouts sent to Oregon from Missouri in 1853 to locate a site for their communal society. She went because, as a young bride, she was determined to be with her husband. *Collection of the Aurora Colony Historical Society, Aurora, Oregon*

From Treasures in the Trunk © 1993 Mary Bywater Cross

Rutledge Hill Press, Nashville, Tennessee

FLORAL **(86″ x 74″, 1875-1900)** Susannah Good
Morris (1822-1915), pioneer of 1851, celebrated her
life doing things in large proportions like the appliqué
blocks of this quilt. Her grandson wrote "My personal
impresson is that she had pieced and quilted well over
a hundred quilts; perhaps all of which she gave away
with the exception of those that she used in the house."
Collection of the Yamhill County Historical Museum

From Treasures in the Trunk © 1993 Mary Bywater Cross

Rutledge Hill Press, Nashville, Tennessee

HEXAGON (80¾″ x 60″, begun 1869, finished 1900)
This well-documented quilt was the work of Abigail
Scott Duniway (1834-1915), early business woman,
journalist, and a women's suffrage leader. She came
over the Oregon Trail in 1852 with her parents and
family. *Collection of the Oregon Historical Society,
Portland, Oregon*

From Treasures in the Trunk © 1993 Mary Bywater Cross

Rutledge Hill Press, Nashville, Tennessee

SUNFLOWER (101″ x 85″, c. 1860) This quilt was made by Matilda Knight Stauffer (1835-1867), a pioneer of 1863 and a member of the Bethel-Aurora Communal Society. The extensive amount of hand piecing and quilting indicates that other members of the Society may have contributed to the quilt's completion. *Private collection*

From Treasures in the Trunk © *1993 Mary Bywater Cross*

Rutledge Hill Press, Nashville, Tennessee

HONEYSUCKLE (94″ x 80″, c. 1850) This appliquéd quilt by the great-great-aunts of Minnie Robison Colver (1880-1960) has two unusual features. The vine border exists on three sides and is absent from one long edge. The wheel motif in the quilting design is associated with migration and leave-taking. *Collection of the Southern Oregon Historical Society, Medford, Oregon*

From Treasures in the Trunk © *1993 Mary Bywater Cross*

Rutledge Hill Press, Nashville, Tennessee

PRINCESS FEATHER (**88″ x 64″, c. 1860**) This quilt was made by Margaret Fuson Lieuallen (1838-1931) and her mother Sarah Moody Fuson (?-1898) in preparation for her marriage and overland journey to Oregon in 1864. *Private collection*

From Treasures in the Trunk © *1993 Mary Bywater Cross*

Rutledge Hill Press, Nashville, Tennessee

WILD GOOSE CHASE VARIATION (84″ x 61″, c. 1865-1880) This hand stitched quilt was made by the widow Sarah Moody Fuson (?-1898) while living in Missouri. The migration theme of movement and change in its strip piecing of triangles is symbolic of her life. She came to Oregon after all of her children had left their Missouri home. *Private collection*

From Treasures in the Trunk © 1993 Mary Bywater Cross

Rutledge Hill Press, Nashville, Tennessee

BASKET (**74″ x 68″, c. 1860s**) The note on the quilt read "Grandma Nancy's quilt, brought from Missouri" when it was found among her granddaughter's belongings after her death. Nancy Callaway Nye (1810-1883) had come West as a widow to join her sons in 1865. The gray-colored fabric is unusual in quilts of this period, leading to speculation it may be a faded purple. *Private collection*

From Treasures in the Trunk © *1993 Mary Bywater Cross*

Rutledge Hill Press, Nashville, Tennessee

PINK AND GREEN (87″ x 71″, c. 1875) This quilt reflects the desire of the members of the Aurora Colony Communal Society to share and work together. There are at least six quilts in the Society's collection with the same color scheme and piecing and quilting patterns. *Collection of the Aurora Colony Historical Society, Aurora, Oregon*

From Treasures in the Trunk © *1993 Mary Bywater Cross*

Rutledge Hill Press, Nashville, Tennessee

FRUIT AND FLOWERS (**89″ x 89″, c. 1855**) This masterpiece appliquéd and stuffwork quilt was made by Mary Carpenter Pickering Bell (1831-1900) in Ohio while waiting for her friend John Bruce Bell, who went to Oregon in 1850. He returned eight years later and they were married in 1861, eventually settling in Iowa. *Collection of the Smithsonian Institution, Washington, D.C.*

From Treasures in the Trunk © *1993 Mary Bywater Cross*

Rutledge Hill Press, Nashville, Tennessee

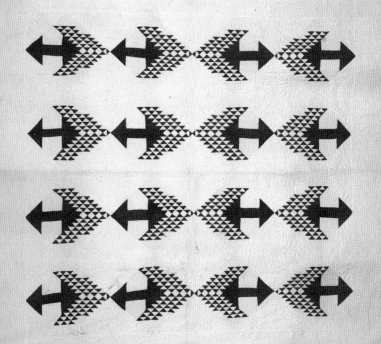

PINE TREE (**80″ x 76″, 1849**) This quilt was made by
Emma and Kate Helman in Ohio as a wedding gift for
their brother Abel Helman prior to his marriage to
Martha Jane Kanaga Helman and their westward
migration. *Collection of the Southern Oregon
Historical Society, Medford, Oregon*

From Treasures in the Trunk © *1993 Mary Bywater Cross*

Rutledge Hill Press, Nashville, Tennessee